THE SCIENTIFIC LIVING SERIES
THE HOW AND WHY SCIENCE BOOKS

SUN SHINE AND RAIN

George Willard Frasier
Helen Dolman MacCracken
Lois Gabel Armstrong
Illustrated by
Guy Brown Wiser

THE L. W. SINGER COMPANY

Syracuse, New York

SUNSHINE

AND RAIN

Bob Looks Up and Down

Look! Look!

Can you find Bob?

Can you see where Bob is?

Bob can see up and down.

Bob looks up.

Bob sees the sky.

The sky is not little.

The sky is big.

Bob looks down.

Bob sees the earth.

The earth is not little.

The earth is big.

Bob looks down.

He can see the earth.

It is big.

Bob can see the water.

The water looks blue.

Bob looks and looks at the earth.

He can see water.

He can see land.

The earth is land and water.

The earth is big.

Bob comes down.

He comes down to the earth.

Bob lives on the land.

You and I live on the land.

We live on the earth.

We can go on the land.

We can go on the water.

We can go in the air.

The earth is land and water and air.

Rain

Mother said, "Come Bob.

Come here.

"See the big clouds in the sky.

"Clouds make rain."

Down comes the rain.

Rain makes the earth wet.

It can not make Bob wet.

Can it make Susan wet?

The Air Is Wet

Bob can not see the sky.

Fog is in the air.

The air is wet.

Fog is not rain.

Is fog water?

See! The Sun

See the blue sky.

The air is warm.

The land is warm.

The sun makes the land warm.

The land makes the air warm.

Snow Comes

See the sun and clouds.

The snow comes from clouds.

The sun warms the snow.

Water comes from snow.

Snow is water.

Big snowflakes are in the air.

Snowflakes are cold.

The sun warms the snowflakes.

The snowflakes go away.

Where do the snowflakes go?

Oh! The Wind

Oh, my! The wind!

I can not play here.

I can not play in the leaves.

The wind makes the leaves go away.

I can see the leaves.

I can not see the wind.

Is the wind here?

Can you see it?

The wind can help you.

It can help on the land.

It can help in the air.

It can help on the water.

It Is Day

Where is the sun?

The sun makes light.

The light helps you see.

It helps you see in the day.

The sun shines on the earth.

It makes the earth warm.

The sun makes you warm.

It helps you grow.

Night Comes

The moon is in the sky.

Light comes from the moon.

The light from the moon

helps you see.

It helps you see at night.

Stars shine in the sky.

You can see the stars at night.

Stars make a little light.

The stars help you see at night.

From Autumn to Autumn

See the big red apples.

Apples are good in autumn.

Down, down the apples come.

Bob and Susan like apples.

Winter is here.

Snow is on the apple tree.

Where are the apples?

Where are the leaves?

Little leaves are on the apple tree.

Flowers are on the apple tree.

Is it autumn?

Is it spring?

The leaves on the apple tree are big.

Little green apples are on the tree.

The warm sun
makes the apples grow.

The apples grow big in summer.

Plants

Plants live on the earth.

The rain helps the plants grow.

The sun helps the plants grow.

What plants do you see?

Some plants grow in the water.

Can you find one?

Some plants grow on the land.

Can you find one?

Some plants have big leaves.

Can you find one?

Some plants have little leaves.

Can you find one?

Animals

Animals live on the earth.

Some animals live on the land.

Some animals live in the water.

What animals do you see?

Some animals have two legs.

Can you find one?

Some animals have four legs.

Can you find one?

Some animals have no legs.

Can you find one?

Find a big animal.

Find a little animal.

Some things live.

Some things do not live.

Plants and animals live.

Find some things that do not live.

A Walk

"Come, Bob and Susan,"
said Father.

"Mother and I are going
for a walk.
You may come, too.

"Autumn is here.
See what you can find."

"Here is something for you,"
said Mother.

"It is something you like.

"You may take one, Susan.

"You may take one, Bob.

"Apples are good in autumn."

34

"Why are the leaves red and yellow?" said Susan.

"Trees grow in spring and summer. They do not grow in autumn," said Mother. "That is why the leaves are red and yellow."

"See the squirrel run
up the tree," said Father.
"It is going to hide something."

"I see one, two, three squirrels,"
said Bob.

"Do squirrels live in trees?"

"Look at that chipmunk,"
said Bob. "What is it doing?"
"The chipmunk is going
to hide something," said Father.
"It will hide something
to eat in winter."

"I see three insects," said Father.

"Can you find the insects I see?"

"Are bees insects?" said Susan.

"I see some bees."

"I see some butterflies," said Bob.

"Are butterflies insects?"

"Yes," said Father.

"Butterflies and bees are insects."

"I see a toad," said Susan.

"Are toads insects?"

"No, Susan," said Father.

"Toads are not insects.

Toads have four legs.

"Insects have six legs.

Look for animals with six legs."

"The grasshopper has six legs,"
said Bob.
"Grasshoppers are insects.
I see four grasshoppers."

"Yes, grasshoppers are insects,"
said Father.
"Butterflies are insects.
Bees are insects.
Grasshoppers are insects."

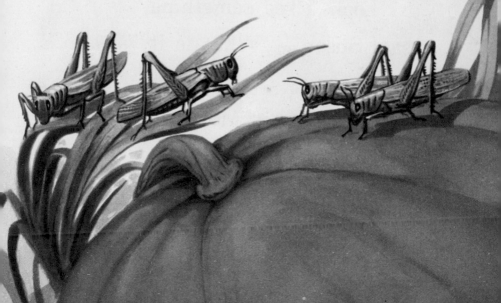

"Look, I see something,"
said Susan. "What is it?"

"You may take it home
with you," said Mother.

"Some day you will see
what is in it.

Some day it will surprise you."

"Here is a turtle in the water,"
said Bob. "May I take it with me?"

"Yes," said Father.
"You may take the turtle with you.
I will take the toad.
Susan has the surprise.
We have three animals
to take home."

"Is the surprise an animal?"
said Bob.

"Yes," said Father.
"The surprise is an insect.
Insects are animals."

"I see a snake!" said Susan.

"Run! Run! Run!"

"Do not run," said Father.

"The snake will not hurt you.

I will take the snake with me."

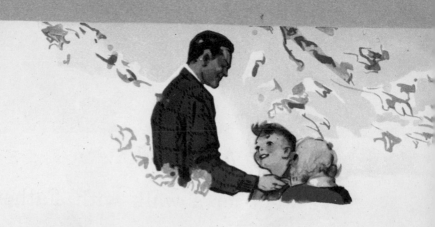

"May we take the animals
to school?" said Bob.

"Will Miss Brown want animals
at school?" said Father.

"Yes," said Susan.
"Miss Brown wants plants
and animals at school.
We have plants at school.
We do not have animals."

"You may take the animals
to school," said Father.

At School

"We went for a walk with Father and Mother," said Susan.

"We have four animals," said Bob. "Here is a toad. Here is a snake."

"A snake!" said Jimmy. "Will it hurt you?"

"No," said Bob. "The snake will not hurt you if you do not hurt it."

"Here is a turtle," said Susan. "And here is a surprise."

"A surprise!" said Miss Brown. "What is the surprise?"

"The surprise is an animal,"
said Susan. "It is an insect."

"What is an insect?"
said Jimmy.

"An insect is an animal
with six legs," said Susan.

"We saw three squirrels and
a chipmunk," said Bob.

"We saw autumn leaves,"
said Susan.

"Thank you, Bob and Susan,"
said Miss Brown.
"We will make homes
for the animals."

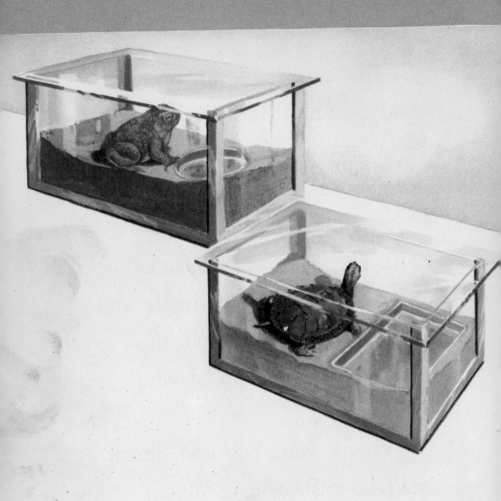

Homes for the Animals

Here are the homes the children
made for the animals.

What will the animals do
in winter?

Will the surprise live on land?

Will it live in water?

Will it fly in the air?

Two Caterpillars

One morning Jimmy saw
a caterpillar.

"Here is a green caterpillar,"
he said.

"I will take it with me.
I will take it to school."

Jimmy made a home
for the green caterpillar.
The caterpillar ate the leaves.
It made a cocoon.
"The cocoon is its winter home,"
said Miss Brown.

Nancy saw a fuzzy animal
on the walk.

"What is it?" said Nancy.
"I will take it to school.
I will see if it will make
a cocoon."

"Here is a fuzzy animal,"
said Nancy. "What is it?"

"It is a caterpillar,"
said Jimmy.

"But it is not green,"
said Nancy.

"Not all caterpillars are green,"
said Miss Brown.

"The fuzzy animal is a caterpillar."

The children made a home
for the fuzzy caterpillar.
It did not eat the leaves.
It did not make a cocoon.
Soon it went under the leaves.
Miss Brown said,
"The caterpillar will live
under the leaves all winter."

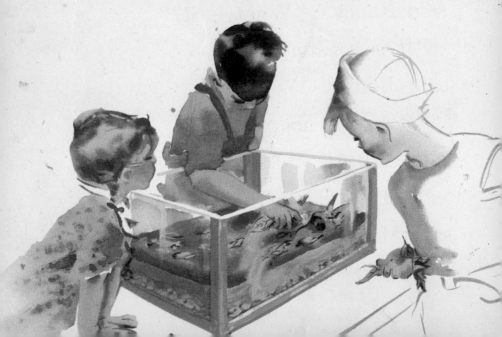

The Surprise

One morning in autumn
Miss Brown said, "Come, children!
"Look at the surprise!
I saw it move.
It is going to open soon!"

"Oh, I saw it move, too,"
said Nancy.

"And I can see it move," said Bob.

"See it open," said Miss Brown.
"Look! You will see something
come out."

"A butterfly!" said Bob.

"A butterfly!" said Nancy.

"The surprise is a butterfly!"

"The butterfly is wet,"
said Nancy.

"It will dry soon,"
said Miss Brown.

"Can it fly?" said Bob.

"When it is dry it can fly.
It will fly away," said Miss Brown.

"Where will the butterfly go?"
said Susan.

"It will go where it is warm,"
said Miss Brown.

"It will fly away for the winter."

Ready for Winter

"The toad is ready for winter,"
said Miss Brown.
"The turtle is ready for winter.
The snake is ready. The squirrel
and the chipmunk are ready.

"Are you ready for winter?
Do you make cocoons?
Do you hide food away?
What makes you warm in winter?"

"We do not make cocoons,"
said Jimmy.
"But we have warm homes.
We have warm clothes, too."

"We do not hide food away,"
said Bob.   "But Mother cans food.
Food will keep in cans."

"Frozen food will keep,"
said Nancy.
"Mother freezes food."

"My mother freezes food, too,"
said Susan.

"We dry food," said Jimmy.
"We dry apples in the sun."

Miss Brown said,
"Food helps keep you warm.
Houses help keep you warm.
Clothes help keep you warm.
You will be ready for winter
when it comes."

Susan's Cold

"Come to breakfast," said Mother.

"Here I come!" said Bob.

"Here I come!" said Susan.

"Ker-choo! Ker-choo! Ker-choo!"

"Are you ready for school?" said Mother.

"I am ready," said Bob.

"I am—ker-choo! ker-choo! ker-choo!" said Susan.

"Oh, Susan," said Mother.
"Come with me.
You may have a cold.
You must not go to school."

"But I want to go to school,"
said Susan.

"Children with colds
must not go to school,"
said Mother. "Other children
can get colds from you."

Susan did not go to school
for three days.

She did not eat with Bob.
She did not play with Bob.
She did not play
with other children.

"You may go to school
this morning," said Mother.
"You do not have a cold.
No one can get a cold
from you now."

"Oh, good," said Susan.
"Now I can eat with you.
I can play with Bob.
I can go to school.
I can play with other children.
Thank you, Mother, thank you."

Ready for School

"Are you ready for school?"
said Mother.

"I will be ready soon,"
said Jimmy.

How did Jimmy get ready
for school?

How do you get ready?

"Breakfast is ready," said Mother.

"I am ready, too," Jimmy said.

Jimmy ate a good breakfast.

What do you eat for breakfast?

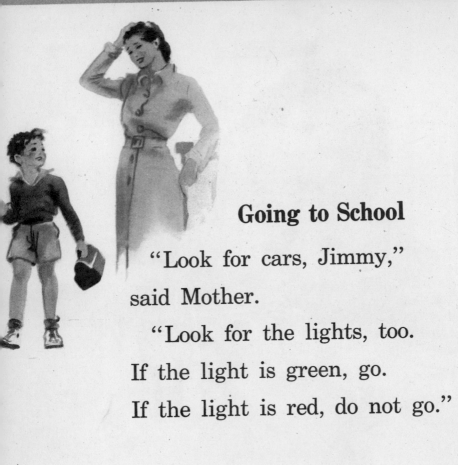

Going to School

"Look for cars, Jimmy,"
said Mother.
"Look for the lights, too.
If the light is green, go.
If the light is red, do not go."

What is Jimmy doing?
Is he safe?

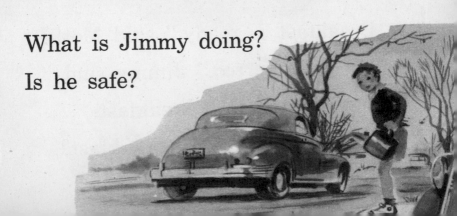

The light is green.

The cars are not going.

Jimmy is safe.   The cars are safe.

Winter Will Soon Be Here

One day we went for a walk.

"The trees have no leaves now,"
said Jimmy.

"The leaves are on the ground.
They are dry and brown.
I like to play in the dry leaves."

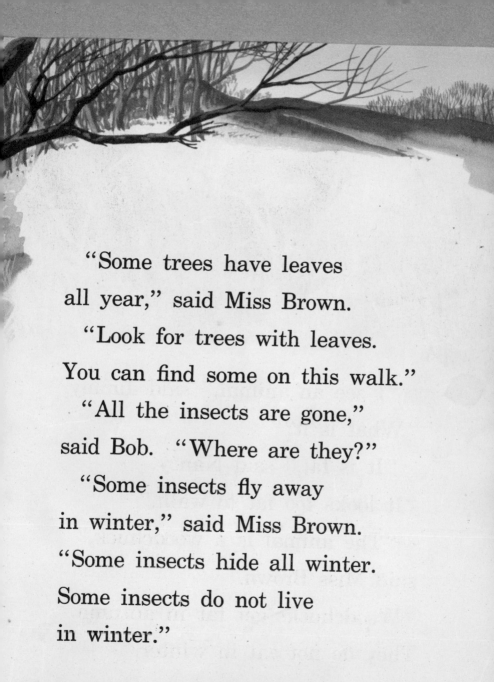

"Some trees have leaves
all year," said Miss Brown.
"Look for trees with leaves.
You can find some on this walk."
"All the insects are gone,"
said Bob. "Where are they?"
"Some insects fly away
in winter," said Miss Brown.
"Some insects hide all winter.
Some insects do not live
in winter."

"I see an animal," said Jimmy.

"What is it?"

"It is fat," said Nancy.

"It looks too fat to walk."

"The animal is a woodchuck,"
said Miss Brown.

"Woodchucks get fat in autumn.
They do not eat in winter."

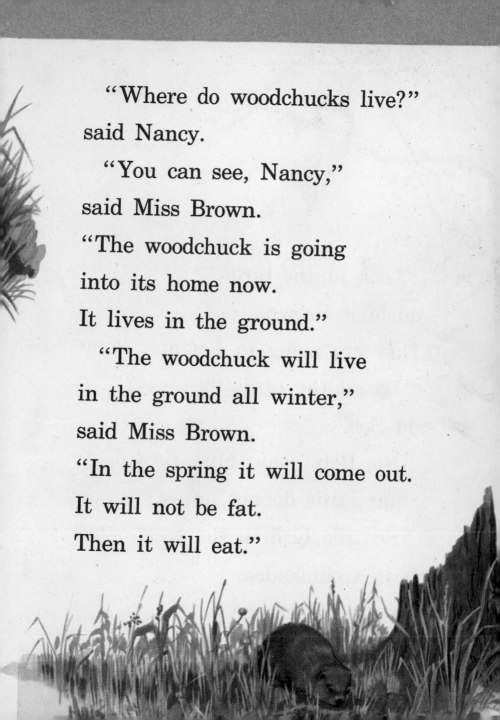

"Where do woodchucks live?"
said Nancy.

"You can see, Nancy,"
said Miss Brown.
"The woodchuck is going
into its home now.
It lives in the ground."

"The woodchuck will live
in the ground all winter,"
said Miss Brown.
"In the spring it will come out.
It will not be fat.
Then it will eat."

"Look at the birds,"
said Miss Brown.
"They are going to a winter home."

"Do all the birds fly away?"
said Bob.

"No, Bob," said Miss Brown.
"Some birds do not fly away.

"See the bird in the tree.
"It is a chickadee.
The chickadee lives here
all year."

"Oh, I see a bird," said Nancy.
"Look, it moves upside down."

"It is an upside down bird,"
said Jimmy.

"The bird is a nuthatch,"
said Miss Brown.
"Nuthatches move upside down."

"Is it a winter bird?" said Susan.

"It lives here all year,"
said Miss Brown.

"I hear a winter bird,"
Miss Brown said.
"Do you hear it?"

"A woodpecker!" said Bob.
"I hear it. I see it, too."

"The woodpecker lives here
all year," said Miss Brown.
"The woodpecker finds food
in the trees."

"What do other birds eat
in winter?" Jimmy said.

"They eat insects and other food,"
said Miss Brown.

"Some birds eat seeds."

"I feed my bird seeds," said Bob.

"We can feed the birds at school,"
said Miss Brown.

The Lunch Counter

This is how we feed the birds.

The birds like the lunch counter.

Chickadees, nuthatches,

and woodpeckers come to eat.

Other birds come

to the lunch counter, too.

What do they eat?

Tracks in the Snow

"I like to make tracks
in the snow," said Bob.
"It is fun to make tracks.
See my tracks, Father?"

"Yes," said Father.
"I see the tracks you made.
I see other animal tracks, too."

Some animals look for food
at night.
Here are the tracks
Bob and Father saw.
What animals made the tracks?

Winter Days

"Come in, children," said Mother.

"It is time to eat."

"May we play after we eat?"
said Susan.

"We like to play in the snow."

"Yes, you may play

after you eat," said Mother.

"You may play if it is light."

Bob and Susan went out to play
after they ate.

"Oh, my," said Bob.
"It is too dark to play now.
The sun has gone down.
We can not see in the dark."

Bob and Susan went
into the house.

"The sun has gone down,"
they said.

"We can not play in the dark."

"The days are short in winter,"
said Mother. "The nights are long.
You may play in the house."

Next morning Mother said,
"Come, children, it is time
to get up."

"It is dark," said Bob.
"I can not find my clothes."

"It is cold," said Susan.
"Where is the sun?"

"You must get up before the sun
is up," said Mother.

"The days are short now.
In summer the days will be long.
The nights will be short."

Ice

Water freezes in winter.

Ice is frozen water.

We have fun on the ice.

Do you?

See the long icicles on the house.

They are frozen water, too.

The sun makes the icicles shine.

The sun makes the icicles get short, too.

Animals in Winter

"What are the caterpillars doing?"
Jimmy said one day.

"The fuzzy caterpillar is
under the leaves," said Bob.

"The green caterpillar is
in its cocoon," said Susan.

"Where is the toad?" said Nancy.

"It is in the ground,"
said Miss Brown.
"It will stay in the ground
a long time.

"The turtle will stay
in the ground, too."

"The snake is out," said Susan.
"Why did the snake come out?"

"The warm sun made the snake
come out," said Miss Brown.

"When will the other animals come out?" said Susan.

"They will not come out before spring," said Miss Brown. "Then the fuzzy caterpillar will make a cocoon."

"What will the green caterpillar do?" said Jimmy.

"You will see when spring comes," said Miss Brown. "It will be fun for you to find out."

Bulbs

"What do you have,
Miss Brown?" said Nancy.

"I have some bulbs," said
Miss Brown. "You may plant
the bulbs. They will grow in water."

The children put the bulbs
into water.

They put stones into the water,
too.

They put some stones
under the bulbs.

Then they put the bulbs
in the dark.

"May we put the bulbs
in the light?" said Nancy
the next morning.

"Bulbs do not grow in one night,"
said Miss Brown.

"They must stay in the dark now.
They will grow soon."

One day Susan said, "The bulbs
are growing now. I see roots
growing under the stones."

"The roots are growing
in the water," said Jimmy.

"Plants must have water before
they will grow," said Miss Brown.
"Roots get water for the plants.
It is time to put the plants
in the light."

The sun shines on the plants.

It makes the leaves grow.

It helps make the flowers open.

"I like the flowers," said Susan.

"May we plant bulbs next year?"

"Yes," said Miss Brown.

"You may plant seeds, too.

Seeds grow into plants."

WORD LIST

In writing this primer, SUNSHINE AND RAIN, the authors have assumed that the child, at the time the book is introduced to him, has learned to read sixty-five words which are found commonly in the most widely-used pre-primers. Those sixty-five words are as follows:

a	did	here	may	run	want
all	do	help	me	said	we
am	down	home	mother	see	went
and	eat	I	my	she	what
are	father	in	no	the	where
at	find	is	not	this	will
away	for	it	oh	three	with
big	get	like	on	to	yellow
blue	go	little	one	too	yes
can	good	look	play	two	you
come	he	make	red	up	

SUNSHINE AND RAIN introduces and teaches 139 other words. 126 of these words are found in the Gates list or the Stone vocabulary lists for primary children. The remaining 13 words are either proper names or necessary science words.

The following is a list of the 139 additional words. The figure preceding each word is the number of the page on which the word is introduced. Not more than two words are introduced on any one page. All variants are counted as new words except when made by the addition of s. The average number of words introduced per page is 1.4. Each word is repeated three or more times within the book.

4 Bob	10 air	14 fog	18 wind
5 sky	11	15 sun	leaves
6 earth		warm	19
7 water	12 rains	16 snow	20 day
8 land	clouds	from	light
9 lives	13 wet	17 snowflakes	21 shines
	Susan	cold	grow

95

22 night
moon

23 stars

24 autumn
apples

25 winter
tree

26 flowers
spring

27 green
summer

28 plants

29 some
have

30 animals

31 legs
four

32 things
that

33 walk
going

34 something
take

35 why
they

36 squirrel
hide

37 chipmunk
doing

38 insects
bees

39 butterflies

40 toad
six

41 grasshopper
has

42 surprise

43 turtle
an

44 snake
hurt

45 school
Miss Brown

46 Jimmy
if

47 saw
thank

48 children
made

49 fly

50 caterpillars
morning

51 ate
cocoon

52 Nancy
fuzzy

53 but

54 soon
under

55 move
open

56 out
butterfly

57 dry
when

58 ready
food

59 clothes
keep

60 frozen
freezes

61 houses

62 breakfast
ker-choo

63 must
other

64

65 now

66 be
how

67

68 cars
safe

69

70 ground

71 year
gone

72 fat
woodchuck

73 into

74 then
birds
chickadee

75 upside
nuthatch

76 hear
woodpecker

77 seeds
feed

78 lunch
counter

79 tracks
fun

80

81

82 time
after

83 dark

84 short
long

85 next
before

86 ice

87 icicles

88

89 stay

90

91 bulbs

92 put
stones

93 growing
roots

94

3793